CELEBRATING BLACK PANTHERS

Celebrating Black Panthers

Walter the Educator

Silent King Books

SILENT KING BOOKS

SKB

Copyright © 2024 by Walter the Educator

All rights reserved. No part of this book may be reproduced in any manner whatsoever without written permission except in the case of brief quotations embodied in critical articles and reviews.

First Printing, 2024

Disclaimer
This book is a literary work; the story is not about specific persons, locations, situations, and/or circumstances unless mentioned in a historical context. Any resemblance to real persons, locations, situations, and/or circumstances is coincidental. This book is for entertainment and informational purposes only. The author and publisher offer this information without warranties expressed or implied. No matter the grounds, neither the author nor the publisher will be accountable for any losses, injuries, or other damages caused by the reader's use of this book. The use of this book acknowledges an understanding and acceptance of this disclaimer.

Celebrating Black Panthers is a little collectible book that belongs to the Little Collectible Book Series by Walter the Educator. Collect them all and more books at WaltertheEducator.com

BLACK PANTHERS

In the heart of shadowed night, the black panther prowls,

Celebrating
Black Panthers

A phantom of the jungle, where the twilight bows.

Celebrating
Black Panthers

Through the thick, emerald canopy, silent paws tread,

Celebrating
Black Panthers

A specter of elegance, in the moonlight's thread.

Celebrating
Black Panthers

Eyes like golden lanterns, piercing the inky shroud,

Celebrating
Black Panthers

Gleam with ancient wisdom, unspoken but loud.

Celebrating
Black Panthers

Whiskers twitch, sensing whispers in the cool, crisp air,

Celebrating
Black Panthers

Every sinew, every muscle, honed with lethal care.

Celebrating
Black Panthers

In the cradle of the wild, where the rivers wind,

Celebrating
Black Panthers

The black panther moves with a grace, one of a kind.

Celebrating
Black Panthers

Each step, a rhythmic heartbeat of the untamed land,

Celebrating
Black Panthers

A testament to the wild's intricate, masterful hand.

Celebrating
Black Panthers

Fur like midnight velvet, absorbing all light,

Celebrating
Black Panthers

A cloak of deepest black, blending into night.

Celebrating
Black Panthers

It's a canvas of mysteries, of secrets untold,

Celebrating
Black Panthers

A symbol of beauty, fierce and bold.

Celebrating
Black Panthers

From the high mountain ranges to the valley below,

Celebrating Black Panthers

Where the silver rivers of the moonlight flow,

Celebrating
Black Panthers

The panther reigns supreme, a regal knight,

Celebrating
Black Panthers

Guarding the jungle realms under the cloak of night.

Celebrating
Black Panthers

In its eyes, a fire of the cosmos burns,

Celebrating
Black Panthers

A spark of the primordial, as the world turns.

Celebrating
Black Panthers

Ancient as the stars, yet ever so spry,

Celebrating
Black Panthers

A guardian of secrets, under the obsidian sky.

Celebrating
Black Panthers

Through the dense foliage, it moves unseen,

Celebrating
Black Panthers

A whisper in the shadows, sleek and lean.

Celebrating
Black Panthers

It's a silent ode to the night, a moving song,

Celebrating
Black Panthers

A creature of twilight, where the strong belong.

Celebrating
Black Panthers

Its roar, a thunderclap in the silent night,

Celebrating
Black Panthers

Echoes through the wilderness, causing hearts to ignite.

Celebrating
Black Panthers

A call to the wild, a summoning to all,

Celebrating
Black Panthers

To heed the power of the night's enthralling call.

Celebrating
Black Panthers

The black panther, a dance of darkness and light,

Celebrating
Black Panthers

A ballet of survival, in the ebony night.

Celebrating
Black Panthers

Each leap, a defiance of the earthly bounds,

Celebrating
Black Panthers

A master of the hunt, where silence resounds.

Celebrating
Black Panthers

In the dawn's first blush, as the night recedes,

Celebrating
Black Panthers

The panther finds solace in the whispering reeds.

Celebrating
Black Panthers

Resting in its lair, where the shadows play,

Celebrating
Black Panthers

Awaiting the return of the night's ballet.

Celebrating
Black Panthers

May its story be told for centuries to come,

Celebrating
Black Panthers

A legend of the jungle, where the wild ones run.

Celebrating
Black Panthers

The black panther, a marvel of nature's grand design,

Celebrating
Black Panthers

A creature of the night, forever divine.

Celebrating
Black Panthers

ABOUT THE CREATOR

Walter the Educator is one of the pseudonyms for Walter Anderson. Formally educated in Chemistry, Business, and Education, he is an educator, an author, a diverse entrepreneur, and he is the son of a disabled war veteran. "Walter the Educator" shares his time between educating and creating. He holds interests and owns several creative projects that entertain, enlighten, enhance, and educate, hoping to inspire and motivate you. Follow, find new works, and stay up to date with
Walter the Educator™ at
WaltertheEducator.com.

www.ingramcontent.com/pod-product-compliance
Lightning Source LLC
LaVergne TN
LVHW012048070526
838201LV00082B/3854